Monarch Butterfly
Migration

By Susan H. Gray

21st Century
Junior Library

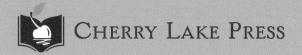

CHERRY LAKE PRESS

Published in the United States of America by Cherry Lake Publishing Group
Ann Arbor, Michigan
www.cherrylakepublishing.com

Reading Adviser: Marla Conn, MS, Ed., Literacy specialist, Read-Ability, Inc.
Content Adviser: Sheila K. Schueller, Ph.D., Lecturer and Academic Program Specialist, University of Michigan
School for Environment & Sustainability
Photo Credits: ©JHVEPhoto/Shutterstock.com, cover; ©Andrea Y. Fraser/Shutterstock.com, 4; ©Tim Herbert/Shutterstock.com, 6;
©Annette Shaff/Shutterstock.com, 8; ©Noradoa/Shutterstock.com, 10; ©Erik Agar/Shutterstock.com, 12; ©Georgi Baird/
Shutterstock.com, 14; ©Media Marketing/Shutterstock.com, 16; ©reisegraf.ch/Shutterstock.com, 18; ©smilesbevie/Shutterstock.com, 20

Cherry Lake Press is an imprint of Cherry Lake Publishing Group.

Library of Congress Cataloging-in-Publication Data

Names: Gray, Susan Heinrichs, author.
Title: Monarch butterfly migration / by Susan H. Gray.
Description: Ann Arbor, Michigan: Cherry Lake Publishing, [2021] | Series:
 Marvelous migrations | Includes index. | Audience: Grades 2-3
Identifiers: LCCN 2020002726 (print) | LCCN 2020002727 (ebook) | ISBN
 9781534168541 (hardcover) | ISBN 9781534170223 (paperback) | ISBN
 9781534172067 (pdf) | ISBN 9781534173903 (ebook)
Subjects: LCSH: Monarch butterfly—Migration—Juvenile literature.
Classification: LCC QL561.D3 G735 2021 (print) | LCC QL561.D3 (ebook) |
 DDC 595.78/91568—dc23
LC record available at https://lccn.loc.gov/2020002726
LC ebook record available at https://lccn.loc.gov/2020002727

Cherry Lake Publishing Group would like to acknowledge the work of the Partnership for 21st Century Learning, a Network of
Battelle for Kids. Please visit http://www.battelleforkids.org/networks/p21 for more information.

Printed in the United States of America
Corporate Graphics

CONTENTS

Each year, hundreds of butterflies are tagged with tracking stickers.

A Flight to Mexico

Monarch butterflies are on the move! Days are growing shorter. The air is becoming cooler. Millions of North American monarchs east of the Rocky

Make a Guess!

Scientists put tiny stickers on monarchs. Each sticker has a different number. This is how they track the butterflies. What are some potential problems with this plan?

Monarch butterflies are known for their distinct orange and black wings.

Mountains are **migrating** south to faraway mountains in Mexico.

Monarchs in the eastern United States and Canada travel as much as 3,000 miles (4,828 kilometers) to Mexico. They fly to **evergreen** forests high in the mountains.

Ask Questions!

Experts knew for years that monarchs flew to Mexico. They searched and searched to find exactly *where* they went. In 1975, they finally discovered the monarchs' stopping place. Why do you think it took so long to find it?

Monarchs collect nectar with their long tongues.

The Big Trip

To fuel their trip, monarchs must stop and feed. As they travel, they spot gardens and fields of wildflowers. They stop and drink **nectar** from the blooms. After feeding, they continue on their way.

At night, the butterflies cluster in trees or shrubs. When morning comes, they **bask** in the sunlight to warm up. Each day, the monarchs travel around 50 to 100 miles

Monarch butterflies swarm around fir trees in Mexico
where they will spend the winter.

(80 to 161 km). The whole trip can take 2 months or more.

Once they reach Mexico, the migrants head straight for the mountains. These are not just any mountains. They are so high they reach into the clouds. The air is cool and foggy.

Evergreen trees that attract monarchs grow there. Millions of the orange-and-black insects cover these trees. Sometimes, branches break under the weight.

Because a monarch caterpillar absorbs the toxins in milkweed,
it is poisonous to **predators**.

Going Back

Mexico is the butterflies' home for the next 5 to 6 months. In March, they begin migrating again. This time, the monarchs fly north.

Think!

Monarchs lay eggs on only one kind of plant—the milkweed. When eggs hatch, tiny caterpillars come out. They eat nothing but milkweed. In time, they develop into butterflies. People love to see monarchs in their yards. What can they do to attract these butterflies to their homes?

A chrysalis is a protective shell that a butterfly hatches from.
A monarch's chrysalis has a gold ring.

They make it to the southern United States and lay millions of eggs throughout the area. After laying their eggs, they die.

The eggs hatch into millions of tiny caterpillars. They are **miniature** eating machines, and they grow quickly. In time, each caterpillar develops into a butterfly. They also continue the journey

Look!

An insect's bold colors can warn predators to stay away. Birds sometimes ignore the monarchs' colors. They eat the caterpillars and butterflies and get sick. Look at pictures of monarch caterpillars and butterflies. What are their warning colors?

You can tell which monarchs are male by two
black spots on their lower wings.

north that their parents started. Along the way, females keep laying eggs.

This cycle repeats several times, each next **generation** moving north. The cycle stops when most of the butterflies have spread into Canada. This last generation of butterflies is special. Next year, they will fly to Mexico.

The monarch migration is the longest for
any insect in North America.

Some Big Mysteries

The monarchs' migration is truly amazing. Adults gather from much of the United States east of the Rocky Mountains and Canada. They fly thousands of miles to a place they have never seen before. They even find the same mountains in Mexico where their great-great-grandparents stayed.

They never make it back, though. It takes several more generations to complete the trip.

You can plant food for monarch butterflies and caterpillars
to help them on their journey!

Scientists have many questions about monarch butterflies. How do they find those Mexican forests? Why do some migrants live for months? Why do others die after just a few weeks? Many big mysteries remain to be solved.

GLOSSARY

bask (BASK) to lie around in the sun for pleasure or to stay warm

evergreen (EV-ur-green) staying green all year

generation (jen-uh-RAY-shuhn) all of the individuals born around the same time

migrating (MYE-grayt-ing) moving from one region to another and back again

miniature (MIN-ee-uh-chur) very small

nectar (NEK-tur) sugary liquid produced by flowers

predators (PRED-uh-turz) animals that hunt and eat other animals

FIND OUT MORE

BOOKS

Aston, Dianna. *A Butterfly Is Patient*. San Francisco, CA: Chronicle Books, 2011.

Marsh, Laura. *Great Migrations: Butterflies*. Washington, DC: National Geographic Children's Books, 2010.

Rabe, Tish. *My, Oh My—A Butterfly!* New York, NY: Random House Children's Books, 2007.

WEBSITES

Kiddle—Monarch (Butterfly) Facts for Kids
https://kids.kiddle.co/Monarch_(butterfly)
Learn all sorts of things about these amazing insects, including their predators and parasites.

National Geographic Kids—Monarch Butterfly
https://kids.nationalgeographic.com/animals/invertebrates/insects/monarch-butterfly
Click through the slideshow and read the article for some great information and photos.

INDEX

ABOUT THE AUTHOR

Susan H. Gray has a master's degree in zoology. She has written more than 170 reference books for children and especially loves writing about animals. Susan lives in Cabot, Arkansas, with her husband, Michael, and many pets.